Animals
Coloring book
for kids
This Coloring book
Belongs to:

Try Your Coloring Pencil Before Coloring

Try Your Coloring Pencil Before Coloring

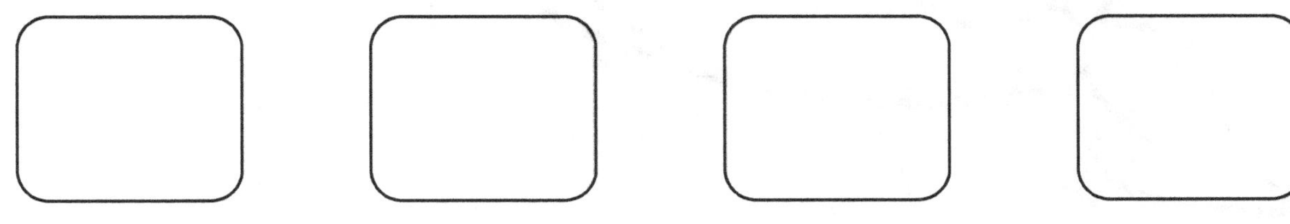

Try Your Coloring Pencil Before Coloring

Try Your Coloring Pencil Before Coloring

Try Your Coloring Pencil Before Coloring

Try Your Coloring Pencil Before Coloring

Try Your Coloring Pencil Before Coloring

Try Your Coloring Pencil Before Coloring

Try Your Coloring Pencil Before Coloring

Try Your Coloring Pencil Before Coloring

Try Your Coloring Pencil Before Coloring

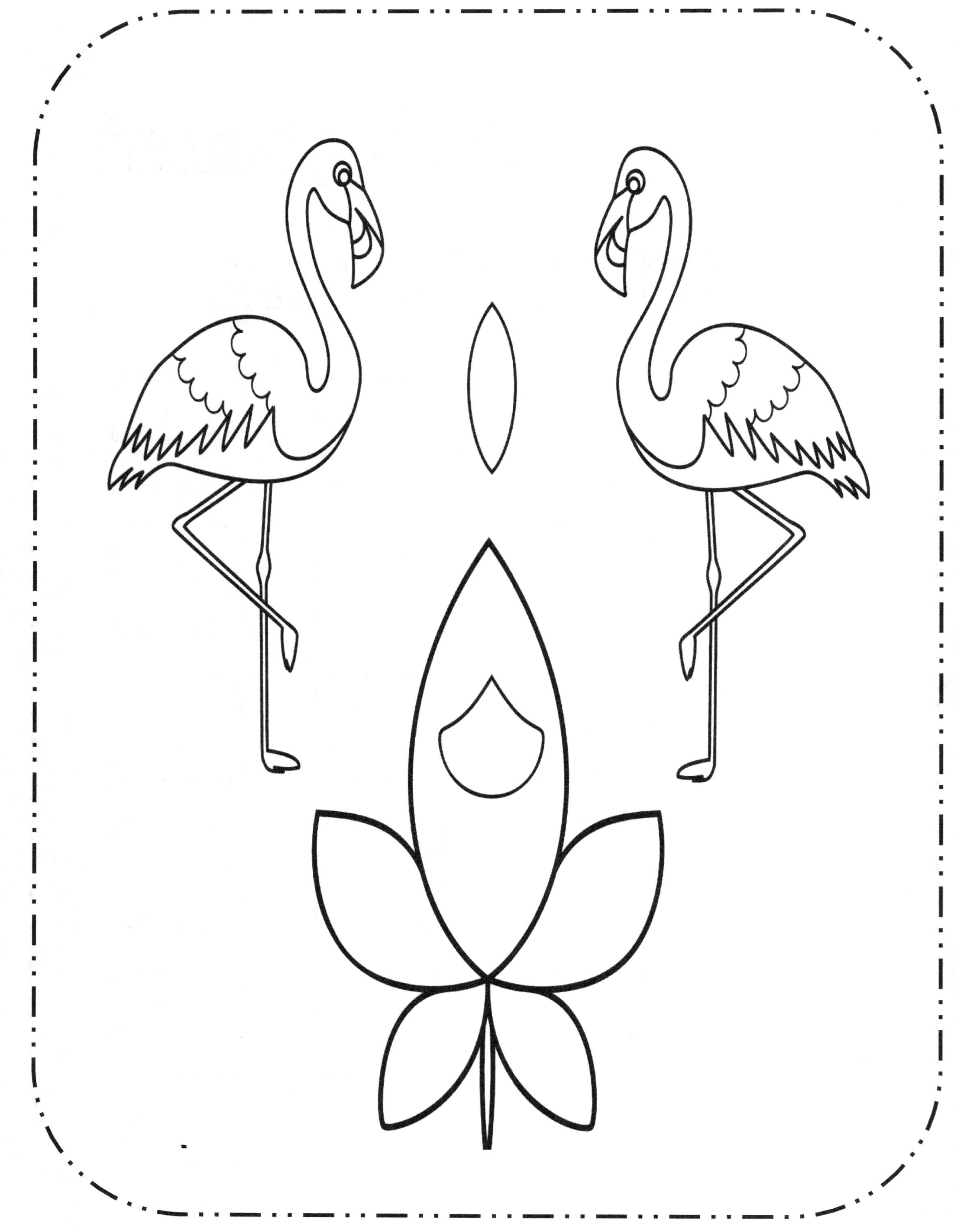

Try Your Coloring Pencil Before Coloring

Try Your Coloring Pencil Before Coloring

Try Your Coloring Pencil Before Coloring

Try Your Coloring Pencil Before Coloring

Try Your Coloring Pencil Before Coloring

Try Your Coloring Pencil Before Coloring

Try Your Coloring Pencil Before Coloring

Try Your Coloring Pencil Before Coloring

Try Your Coloring Pencil Before Coloring

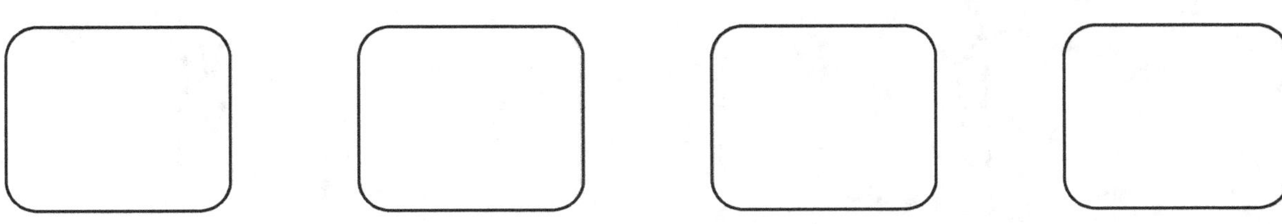

Try Your Coloring Pencil Before Coloring

Try Your Coloring Pencil

Before Coloring

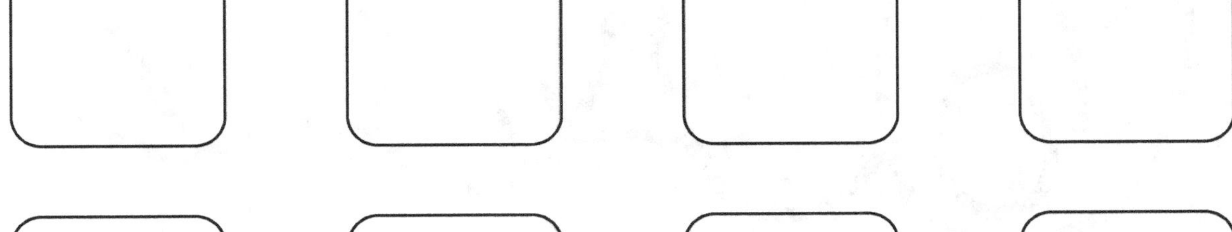
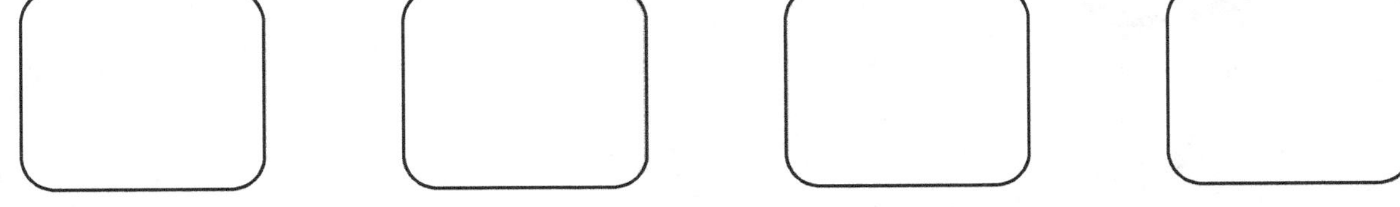

Try Your Coloring Pencil Before Coloring

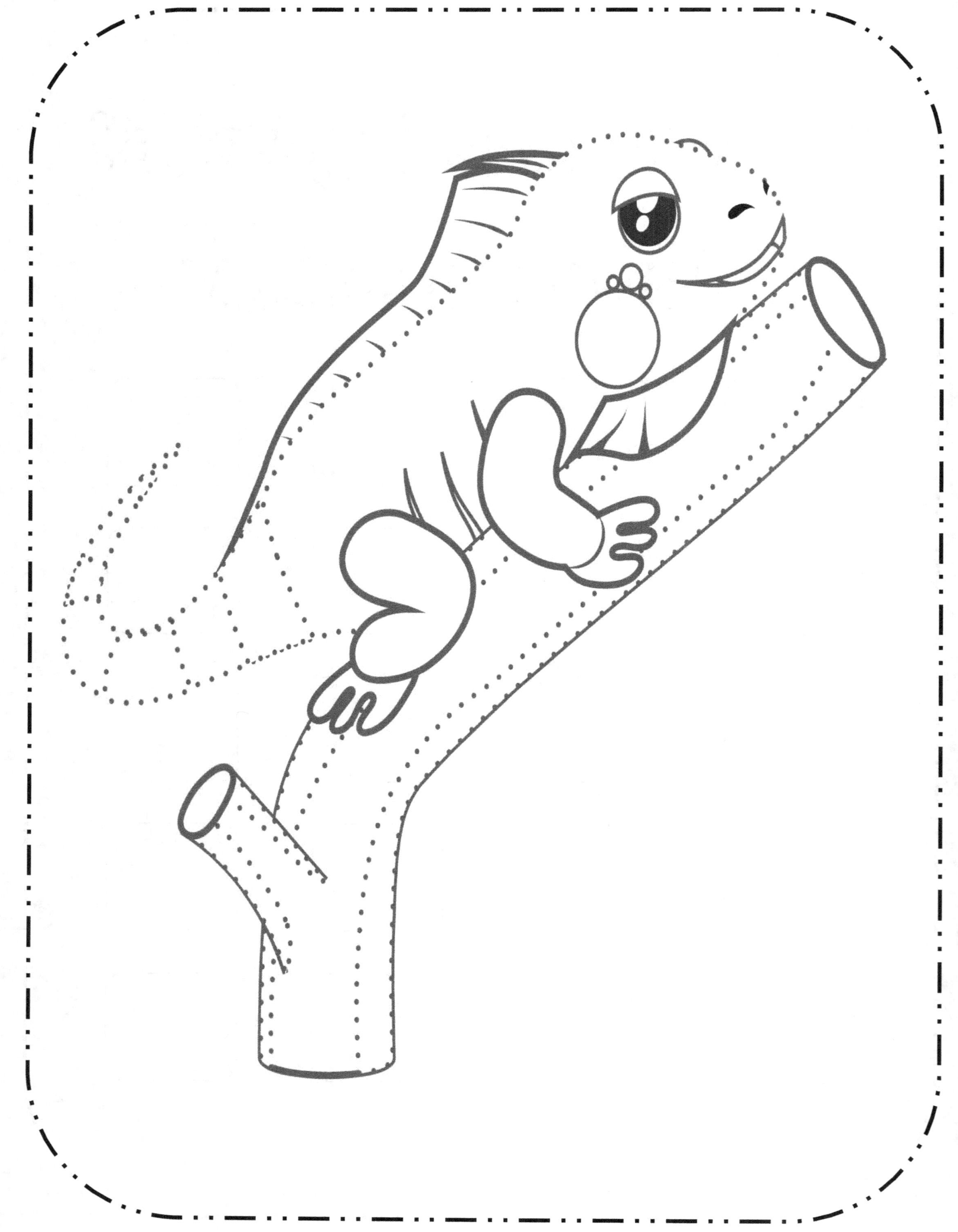

Try Your Coloring Pencil Before Coloring

Try Your Coloring Pencil Before Coloring

Try Your Coloring Pencil Before Coloring

Try Your Coloring Pencil Before Coloring

Try Your Coloring Pencil Before Coloring

Try Your Coloring Pencil Before Coloring

Try Your Coloring Pencil Before Coloring

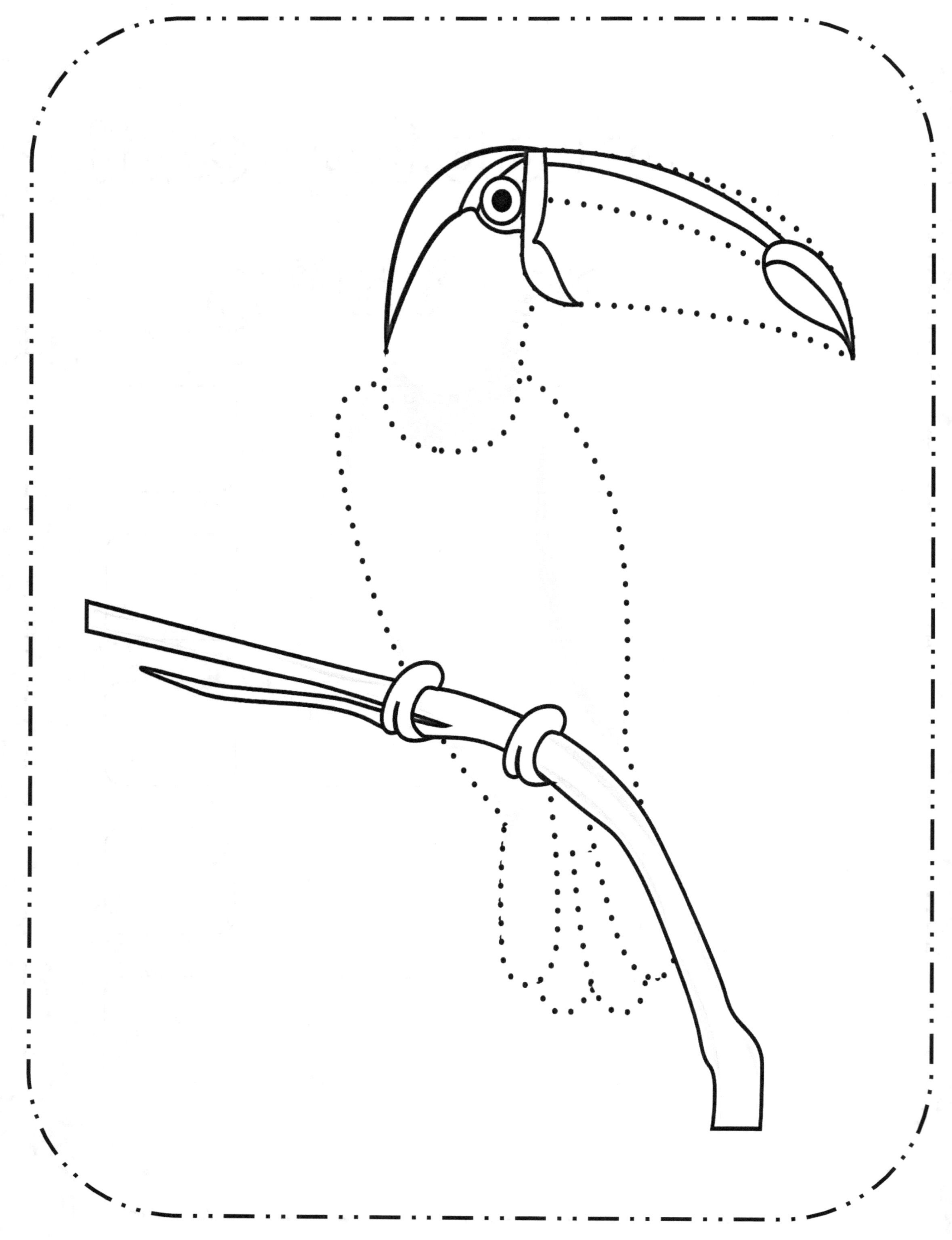

Try Your Coloring Pencil Before Coloring

Try Your Coloring Pencil Before Coloring

Try Your Coloring Pencil Before Coloring

Try Your Coloring Pencil Before Coloring

Try Your Coloring Pencil Before Coloring

Try Your Coloring Pencil Before Coloring